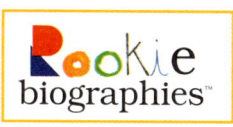

Amelia Earhart

By Wil Mara

Consultants
Nanci R. Vargus, Ed.D.
Primary Multiage Teacher
Decatur Township Schools, Indianapolis, Indiana

Katharine A. Kane, Reading Specialist
Former Language Arts Coordinator
San Diego County Office of Education

Children's Press®
A Division of Scholastic Inc.
New York Toronto London Auckland Sydney
Mexico City New Delhi Hong Kong
Danbury, Connecticut

Designer: Herman Adler Design
Photo Researcher: Caroline Anderson
The photo on the cover shows Amelia Earhart.

Library of Congress Cataloging-in-Publication Data

Mara, Wil.
 Amelia Earhart / by Wil Mara.
    p. cm. — (Rookie biographies)
Summary: Provides an easy-to-read introduction to the life of Amelia Earhart.
Includes index.
   ISBN 0-516-22522-7 (lib. bdg.)   0-516-27338-8 (pbk.)
   1. Earhart, Amelia, 1897-1937—Juvenile literature. 2. Air pilots—United States—Biography—Juvenile literature. 3. Women air pilots—United States—Biography—Juvenile literature. [1. Earhart, Amelia, 1897-1937. 2. Air pilots. 3. Women—Biography.] I. Title. II. Rookie biography.
  TL540.E3 M333 2002
  629.13'092—dc21
                         2001008315

©2002 Children's Press
A Division of Scholastic Inc.
All rights reserved. Published simultaneously in Canada.
Printed in Mexico.

CHILDREN'S PRESS, AND ROOKIE BIOGRAPHIES™, and associated logos are trademarks and or registered trademarks of Grolier Publishing Co., Inc. SCHOLASTIC and associated logos are trademarks and or registered trademarks of Scholastic Inc.
    4 5 6 7 8 9 10 R 11 10 09 08 07 06

Do you ever dream of flying an airplane?

Amelia Earhart did. She was the first woman to fly alone across the Atlantic Ocean.

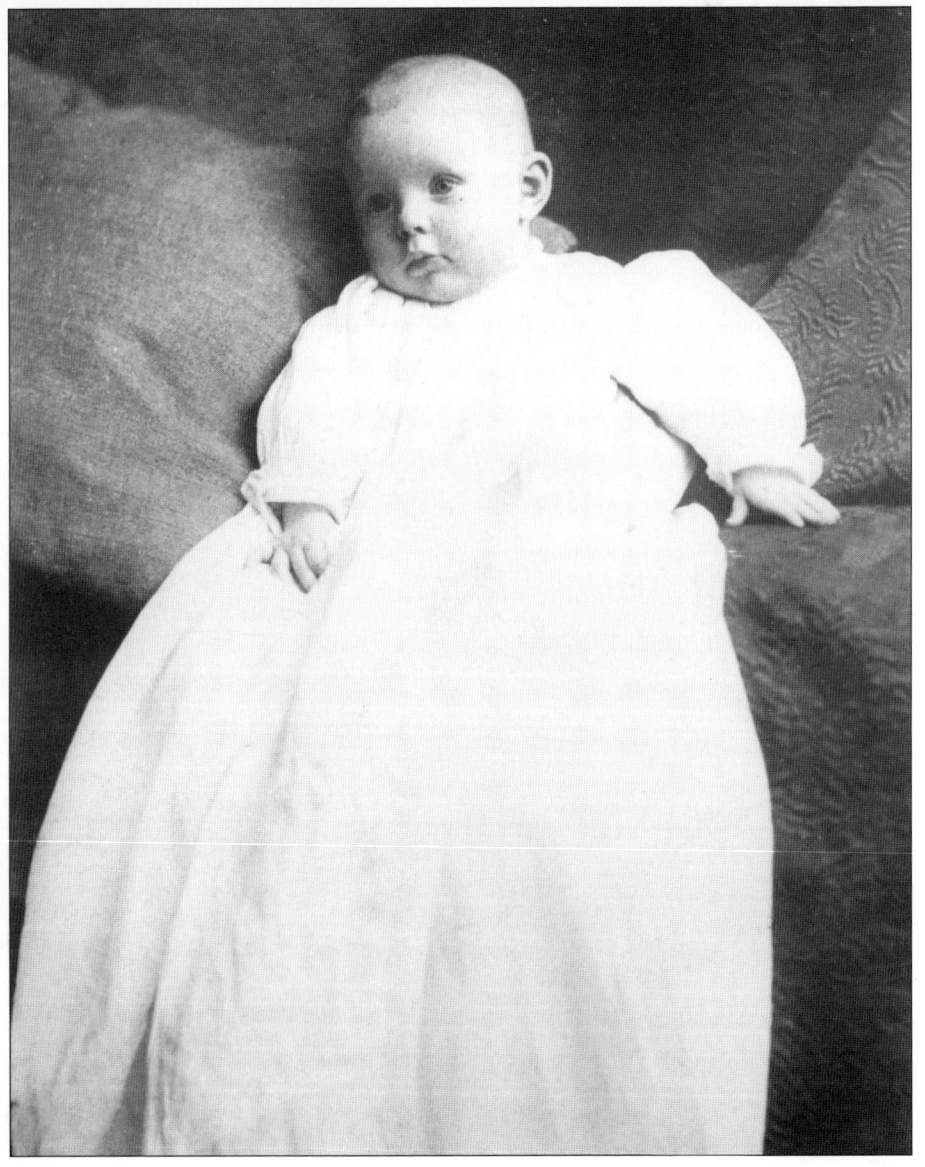

Earhart was born on July 24, 1897, in her grandparents' house in Atchison, Kansas.

From the beginning, Earhart was not afraid to do the same things as boys.

She played most sports. She climbed trees. She even liked to hunt in the woods!

As a young woman, Earhart learned to be a nurse.

Then she went to Canada to help soldiers who had been hurt during World War I.

Earhart went to live with her parents in California in 1920. While she was there, she took her first ride in an airplane.

After that, Earhart knew she wanted to be a pilot. Soon she was taking flying lessons.

Earhart wanted to do things no woman had ever done before.

The first thing she did was fly higher than any other woman pilot. She took her plane up to 14,000 feet (4,300 meters). That's higher than some clouds!

A man named George Putnam wanted to help Earhart become famous as a woman pilot. He asked her to be the first woman to fly across the Atlantic Ocean.

Earhart said yes. She went as a passenger with two other pilots, Wilmer Stultz and Louis "Slim" Gordon.

The newspapers printed stories about Earhart's flight. She was in a big parade, too.

After that, Earhart wrote a book about flying. In 1931, she married George Putnam.

Over the next few years, Earhart was the pilot on many flights that were very dangerous.

Once she flew from Hawaii to California. Many pilots had died trying to make this flight. A crowd of people greeted her after she landed.

Earhart flew across the Atlantic Ocean again in 1932. She was the first woman to make this flight alone.

She also started a club for women pilots. It was called the "Ninety Nines" because there were 99 members when the club began.

By 1937, Earhart had been flying for sixteen years. She was ready to stop, but first she wanted to make one more big flight.

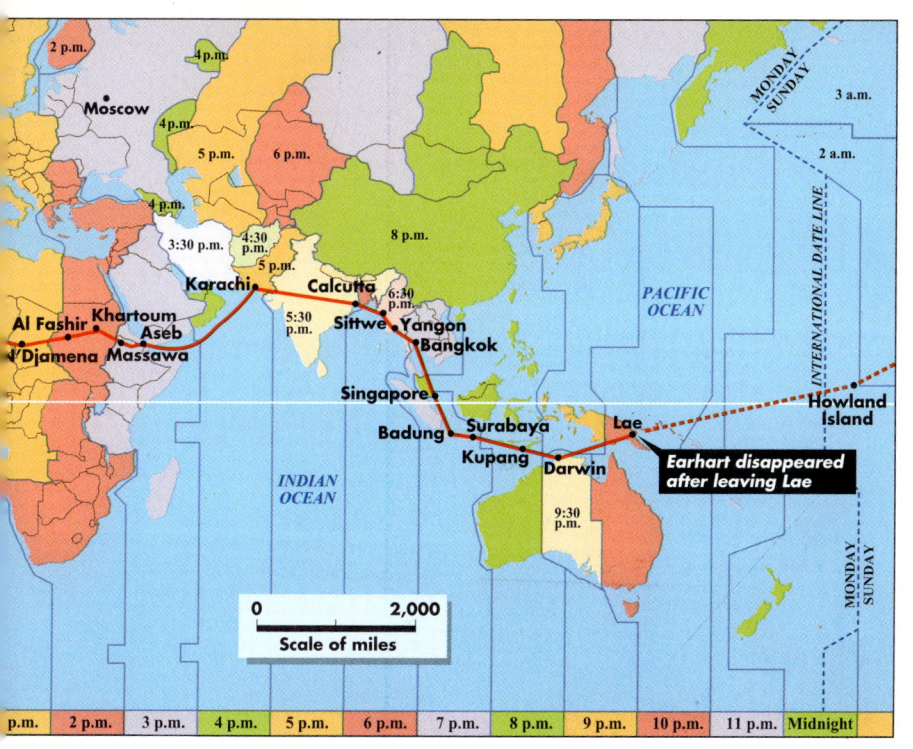

This time she wanted to fly around the world. This map shows where she planned to fly.

Fred Noonan flew with Earhart. They started their trip from Florida in the United States on May 21, 1937. They flew over the Atlantic Ocean and traveled as far as Lae, New Guinea, in the Pacific Ocean.

Then on July 2, their plane disappeared near Howland Island.

No one ever found Amelia Earhart, Fred Noonan, or their plane.

Amelia Earhart proved that a person can do amazing things if he or she is brave enough to try.

Words You Know

airplane

Amelia Earhart

Ninety Nines

Fred Noonan

nurse

parade

pilot

George Putnam

Index

airplanes, 3, 4, 12, 13, 14, 15, 21, 26, 29
Atlantic Ocean, 5, 16, 22, 26
birth, 7
California, 12, 20
Canada, 11
disappearance, 26
flights, 18, 20, 22, 24-25
Florida, 26
Gordon, Louis "Slim," 16, 17, 18
Hawaii, 20
Howland Island, 26
Kansas, 7
map, 24-25
marriage, 19
New Guinea, 26
"Ninety Nines," 23
Noonan, Fred, 26, 27, 29
nurses, 11
Pacific Ocean, 26
parades, 18, 28
pilots, 12, 15, 16, 20, 23
Putnam, George, 16, 19
soldiers, 11
sports, 9
Stultz, Wilmer, 16, 17, 18
women, 5, 15, 16, 22, 23
World War I, 11

About the Author

Wil Mara has written more than fifty books. His works include both fiction and nonfiction for children and adults. He lives with his wife and three daughters in northern New Jersey.

Photo Credits

Photographs © 2002: AP/Wide World Photos: 17, 27, 30 bottom right; Atchison County Kansas Historical Society: 8; Corbis Images/Underwood & Underwood: 18; Franklin Watts/Children's Press: 7; Hulton Archive/Getty Images: 3 (Lambert Studios), 19, 31 bottom right (New York Times Co.), 22; National Air and Space Museum: 21, 30 top left; Purdue University: 13, 31 bottom left; Seaver Center for Western History Research, Los Angeles County Museum of Natural History: 10, 31 top left; Smithsonian Institution, Washington, DC: 6; SODA: 24, 25 (James McMahon) cover (Purdue University); Superstock, Inc.: 4, 30 top right; The Schlesinger Library, Radcliffe Institute, Harvard University: 9, 14, 23, 28, 30 bottom left, 31 top right.